Giovanni

by Lynn Nicastro

Archway Publishing books may be ordered through booksellers or by contacting:

Archway Publishing
1663 Liberty Drive
Bloomington, IN 47403
www.archwaypublishing.com
844-669-3957

Interior Image Credit: Jean Nicastro

ISBN: 978-1-6657-4579-6 (sc)
ISBN: 978-1-6657-4580-2 (e)

Library of Congress Control Number: 2023911261

Print information available on the last page.

Archway Publishing rev. date: 6/23/2023

INTRODUCTION

I came down from heaven and shared
a lifetime of happiness with my family.
This is my story...

They picked me up today and I am so happy to meet the other animals here and be in my new home! I've gotten so many kisses already and feel so loved.

I just woke up from a nice nap, time to play with my favorite toys!

Come down here kitty, I want to play
and I'm too little to climb the stairs yet.

It's Christmas time and I find it fascinating watching the train go round and round under the tree.

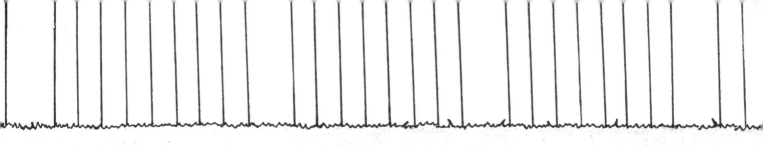

I have so much fun in the yard and being outside in the summer weather! I like playing fetch and have a great time running around.

It's exciting going for walks with mom! Everyday is a great adventure seeing other dogs, people, and sniffing everything in my path. Then, when we get back home, I get a treat.

I miss my family when I can't go with them, so I patiently wait by the window until they get home. When I see the car pull in the driveway, I run to the door and am so excited to see them.

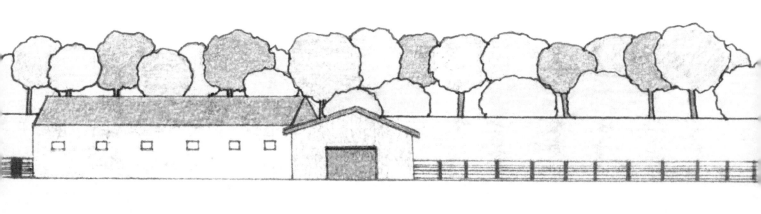

During the summer, going for rides in the car is the best! Today, I saw these beautiful horses much bigger than me.

Time has gone by so fast. It's been almost 15 years with so much fun and happiness. I'm not feeling well now, and soon I will have to say goodbye. I spend most of my time napping and cuddling with my mom.

Hi Jesus, I'm so happy to see you in heaven. My mom was so sad when I left and I hope she knows I love her.

I'm your angel now mom and our hearts will be together forever.

Love, Giovanni

Our pets bring such happiness and unconditional love into our lives. It is very sad to lose them but we are so lucky to have our special friends watching over us in heaven.

Printed in the United States
by Baker & Taylor Publisher Services